Succes[sful]
Proble[m]
Solving *in a week*

Gareth Lewis

Headway · Hodder & Stoughton

Acknowledgements

The author and publishers would like to thank Seven Towns plc for the use of the Rubik's Cube on the cover.

British Library Cataloguing in Publication Data
A catalogue for this title is available from the British Library

ISBN 0 340 64761 2

First published 1995
Impression number 10 9   8 7   6   5   4   3   2   1
Year   1999 1998 1997 1996 1995

Typeset by Multiplex Techniques Ltd, St Mary Cray, Kent.
Printed in Great Britain for Hodder & Stoughton Educational, a division of Hodder Headline Plc, 338 Euston Road, London NW1 3BH by Redwood Books, Trowbridge, Wiltshire.

the Institute of Management

F O U N D A T I O N

The Institute of Management (IM) is at the forefront of management development and best management practice. The Institute embraces all levels of management from students to chief executives. It provides a unique portfolio of services for all managers, enabling them to develop skills and achieve management excellence.

For information on the benefits of membership, please contact:

Department HS
Institute of Management
Cottingham Road
Corby
Northants NN17 1TT

Tel: 01536 204222
Fax: 01536 201651

This series is commissioned by the Institute of Management Foundation.

C O N T E N T S

We rarely go through a day at work when we don't have a few problems to solve. In our challenging working environment we need to tackle ever more complex problems.

This book describes in detail the nature of the kinds of problems we regularly encounter, and how problem situations differ from decision situations.

It provides a model for a systematic approach to the business of solving problems, and covers the tools and techniques, as well as the skills necessary to be effective.

Sunday	Problems, problems
Monday	A problem-solving model
Tuesday	The tools of the trade
Wednesday	The Kepner–Tregoe approach
Thursday	People and problems
Friday	Skills of problem-solving
Saturday	Thinking styles

Problems, problems

Most of this book will be about the concepts and processes involved in solving problems. Before we can explore that, however, we need to look at what problems are – and what they are not. To be able to apply any kind of systematic approach to the business of solving problems, we need to be clear about when and where it is appropriate to do so.

So today, we shall look at:

- The business context
- What are problems?
- Types of problem

The business context

The environment in which we live and work is undergoing radical changes. These changes affect almost every aspect of our working lives, from the competitive market-place, through the kinds of things we do, to the way that we do them.

It has been said that we live in times of turbulent change and that the pace of this change is increasing. We have to run ever faster to stand still. The working environment for most people is becoming more complex and more unpredictable.

Within the fairly recent past, we have relied on a level of stability, coupled with a certain amount of incremental change that allowed businesses to adjust and improve, usually at a comfortable rate, and then to consolidate over a period of time. This kind of incremental change is shown in the first diagram below. These days, it seems, the changes are on a bigger scale, and they are happening more frequently with little time for recovery or consolidation. This discontinuous type of change, or paradigm shift, is shown in the second of the diagrams below.

Incremental change   Discontinuous change

Many of you will have been through the 'Customer is King' revolution, then on to the 'Total Quality' revolution, only to be followed immediately by the 'Business Process Re-engineering' revolution, and all this accompanied by the associated organisational changes, culture changes and market shifts.

In this more complex and fast-changing world, not only is there more that can go wrong, but constant change and adaptation at the deepest levels mean that we have constantly to: *adjust, shift, improve, put right, change, re-engineer and reinvent,* in order to cope with the world about us.

This causes problems at the macro as well as the micro level. It is true to say that we need to be problem-solvers to survive. The working environment, for most people, *means* problems.

Unpredictability, and even chaos, now seem to be the order of the day. In terms of problems, this means that we are faced with:

- More problems – with more complex work situations and incremental change
- Bigger problems – with paradigm changes, re-engineering, etc.
- Different classes of problems – with the coming of the information age, virtual organisations, etc.

These require us to acquire the tools to deal with the everyday problems of diagnosis, maintenance and improvement, but also to develop new tools to deal with turbulence and change, such as creativity, flexibility, 'thinking out of the box'.

What are problems?

For most of us, we know only too well what problems are, and this may seem a trivial question. But ordinary language, and the practice of many writers on the subject, treat almost any situation as a problem. Some of the words that are frequently used, almost interchangeably with 'problem', are:

concerns	challenges
questions	enigmas
mysteries	hindrances

| predicaments | puzzles |
| difficulties | opportunities |

We also use the term 'problem' to cover a very wide range of situations:

- He's causing us all sorts of problems at the moment
- This photocopier has never worked properly
- I don't know which car to buy
- The problem with him is...
- Where are my keys?
- Our meetings are a waste of time
- How can I get this project finished on time?

Problem-solving and decision-making

Problem-solving and decision-making are often confused, and sometimes treated as if they were interchangeable terms. The reason for this is that decisions are often required as a result of problem-solving, and problem situations are often bound up with decision situations.

It is important to make a distinction between situations which require problem-solving techniques and those which require decision-making techniques, because the techniques and tools are quite different.

Decision-making is required when it is necessary to evaluate and select options.

There are many situations where we say something like:

I don't know what to do about replacing the company cars...

Although we may call this a problem, in fact it is more useful, in our terms, to call it a difficulty. What is required here is to make a choice, and the techniques and tools of decision-making are required.

Another typical situation, often called a problem, is:

Stan is underperforming...

This is a situation that will clearly require some decision analysis, decisions and action. But is it a problem?

The answer to that is that if we don't know why Stan is underperforming, then this unknown makes this a problem. It will be necessary to find out why Stan is underperforming, before applying the appropriate remedial action.

This illustrates two important points. First, many situations come with a problem and a decision component. (However, it is possible to have a problem without need of a decision, and a decision without a problem attached.) Some problems require decisions (and decision-making processes) to 'solve' or complete them, and others do not.

Second, if problems and decisions are bound together, it is important to deal with the problem component before the decision-making component. The reason for this is that if we don't, we can't make informed decisions, and we are likely to select a decision which ignores the cause of the problem.

The diagram illustrates that any situation can have varying proportions of problem and decision components.

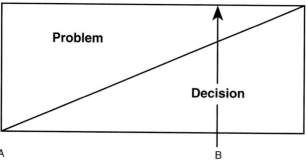

Problem

Decision

A   B

Any vertical line will define the respective proportions. So at point A, there is 100% problem with no decision attached. At point B there is 75% decision, 25% problem (perhaps like the problem with Stan).

The next time you tackle a problem, it is worth giving some thought to the proportions of decision and problem involved.

What should be noticed is that in the problem part of the situation there is an element of uncertainty or the unknown which needs to be tackled. It is this which characterises all problem situations.

Let us summarise these differences.

We know that in decision situations we have:

In decision-making we are answering the question **what**?

In problem-solving we have:

In problem-solving we are answering the question **why**?

So we can define a problem as:

A situation of uncertainty with potential or actual sub-optimal outcomes.

Uncertainty Problem situations are always characterised by an element of uncertainty. The uncertainty is usually around the cause–effect processes involved.

Sub-optimal outcomes The observed (or expected) effects deviate from required standards.

Potential or actual Problems can be prospective as well as retrospective.

So problem-solving is:

The analysis of cause–effect processes in situations of uncertainty with potential or actual sub-optimal outcomes.

There is one further distinction that we should make to complete our description of what problems are.

If you were to list a number of the problems you have had over the last few years, you would probably notice that there is a wide variety of situations that we classify as problems.

The first thing to do is to take out those that we have now classified as decisions (the difficulties).

It is quite likely that there will still be a good variety, and of course, each one is individual and different. However, we can simplify by classifying problems into types.

There are a number of ways of doing this.

Types of problem

Kepner and Tregoe made a very clear distinction between problem-solving and decision-making. They argued that problems arose in situations where there were undesirable outcomes, but where the cause was unidentified.

They defined a problem as:

A deviation from a norm or expectation of unknown cause.

They considered a problem solved when the unidentified cause had been tracked down. They then developed rigorous techniques for solving such problems, which they called problem analysis.

This approach has two major advantages:

1 It clearly separates problem analysis from decision analysis
2 It puts problem-solving firmly into the scientific method.

We shall look in more detail at their technique later in the week.

PS and PF problems
The Kepner–Tregoe definition of a problem is what we would call a 'Problem to solve' or 'PS-type' problem.

However, there are some types of problems that do not fit very neatly into their categorisation. What we need is a definition of problems that is broad enough to cover many of the diverse and complex situations that people face at work, whilst being able to make the everyday language distinction between problems and decisions.

The sorts of problems that do not fit this interpretation include:

- Design-led, or future-oriented problems
- Problems of 'how to...'
- 'How does that work...' problems

Let us give an example:

If we want to put traffic lights at the road junction shown in the diagram, how should they be phased and timed?

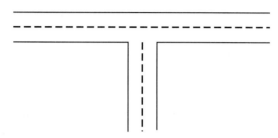

At first examination, this may seem like a decision situation, and indeed, there will be a need to make some decisions eventually. However, before we can do that we need to examine how the system works. There is some uncertainty about the complex relationships of the variables involved. This kind of cause–effect analysis is problem-solving, not decision-making.

In fact, in our problem–decision diagram, this one is indicated by the arrow.

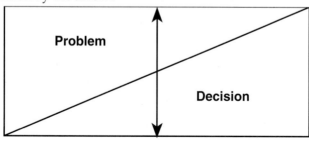

But this kind of problem analysis is not just the tracking down of the unknown cause of some malfunction. Therefore, the Kepner–Tregoe definition (and therefore their techniques) would not work here.

This kind of problem we call a 'Problem to find', or 'PF-type' problem.

In fact, almost any type of problem that is not just the retrospective identification of an unknown cause of a malfunction is a PF-type problem.

Let us look at the notion of norm. Rigid systems like Kepner–Tregoe tend to work well with specific classes of problems, but the systematisation requires a rigid adherence to a binary state of affairs – right or wrong, fixed or broken. Many things in life, however, exist somewhere on the continuum between these two states.

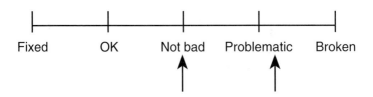

A problem like, 'This machine is not working properly', is at the right-hand end of this continuum, and probably has a single, identifiable cause. It is therefore a PS-type problem.

However, many problems are more fuzzy and indistinct than this. A problem like, 'Our meetings waste time and don't achieve much', might be somewhere between the two arrows shown. The problem might not have a single, identifiable cause, but a complex web of causes and influences. This would make it a PF-type problem.

Finally, problems need not always occur when things go wrong. Therefore problem-solving is sometimes, but not always, about finding causes.

What factors make a successful sales interview?

This is a legitimate problem, but will not be 'solved' by looking for causes. It is a PF-type problem which needs an analysis of the complex relationships between the variables.

Summary

Today, we have looked at definitions and types of problems. We have made the vital distinction between problem situations and decision situations. We have come up with a working definition of problem-solving for our purposes:

The analysis of cause–effect processes in situations of uncertainty with potential or actual sub-optimal outcomes.

We have also identified two types of problems: 'Problems to solve' or 'PS-type' problems – where solving the problem means identifying the unknown cause of some malfunction; and 'Problems to find' or 'PF-type problems' – which may involve analysis of uncertainty in cause–effect relationships in wider contexts.

Tomorrow we will go on to look at the processes of and present a model for problem-solving.

A problem-solving model

Today we will examine the processes involved in problem-solving, and set out a systematic model for the solving of problems.

We will consider:

- Problem-solving as a process
- The 4A model of problem-solving

In certain specific problem situations, a few lucky people can look at the problem and immediately propose a brilliant solution, as if by magic. This astounding party trick happens very rarely. Ninety-nine per cent of the time problem-solving is not like this – if only because it is harder work!

Problems are rarely solved in a single 'hit', as if a light was suddenly turned on. Even in the special cases, the solution appears to arrive quickly because the cogitation that preceded it is hidden (sometimes even to the solver), or because long experience has provided the solution previously.

Imagine taking your car to a garage. The mechanic listens to the spluttering and tapping noises, listens to your description, and immediately diagnoses the problem. The reason he can do this is because he has built up associations and chains of reasoning and connection from many similar past experiences. Even then, you would expect that he checks out and verifies his guess.

Problem-solving as process

The point here is that problem-solving is not just waiting for the light to go on. It is the application of logic, reasoning, judgement and information analysis to situations of uncertainty. It is a structured sequence or process of asking questions. It needs to be ordered and systematic.

This is not to say that there is no room for creativity in problem-solving. Clearly there is, and we shall talk about the balance of scientific or analytic skills and the creative tomorrow.

But in order to encompass both these aspects of our skills there has to be a systematic and structured approach.

Heuristic approaches to the solving of problems, or dealing with difficult ideas have been around for a long time. The ancient Greeks first applied themselves to such rational approaches. Plato and Socrates were the first to reference the testing of propositions. Later philosophers developed systematic ideas on cause and effect (e.g. the English philosopher, David Hume).

Mathematicians and scientists have contributed to the development of universal methods for solving problems. Newton framed his laws of action and reaction as a set of rules for describing cause and effect processes in the natural world.

The term that was applied to the rules of discovery and invention was 'heuristic'. It has been used in rather a vague way. The term and the systematic approach has been developed and used mostly by mathematicians from the time of René Descartes. This century, the mathematician, G. Polya, in his famous book, *How to Solve It* (Penguin, 1990), set out a systematic approach to the solving of problems in his field, with the intention of being able to teach, or to help students to learn the skills of solving problems in the mathematical domain.

We can learn a great deal from this approach, although, of course, problems in a business or working context are not exactly the same as mathematical ones. However, the requirements of a structured approach remain the same. His approach does emphasise a number of features that are characteristic of any systematic approach to solving problems.

1 Problem-solving is an ordered sequence – a process.
2 Processes are based on the asking of relevant questions and the collection and analysis of information.
3 Merely learning or applying a set of rules mechanically will not solve difficult problems, or make you into a good problem-solver. They are a basis, a framework, but experience and skill are developed by practice, determination, and some less scientific qualities – like creativity.

Research has shown that successful problem-solving is about more than just acquiring large amounts of information. Good problem-solvers are investigators, and this implies more than just the availability of information.

Of course there are limitations to the scientific approach:

- The real world is not like the world of philosophical ideas or mathematics.
- It is an ordered approach and the skills have to be learned and honed. There can be no formula which will substitute for experience, knowledge and creativity.
- Much of our knowledge and achievement comes from the inductive or practical approach. From the skill of the ancient Egyptians in making dams and pyramids, to the engineering feats of the nineteenth century, there have been pragmatic, 'learned on the hoof', trial and error methods of tackling problems.

However, much of our success and achievement over the centuries is also due to our ability to model the world and its processes. We make sense of our world, and that includes the business environment, by imposing order and structure on it. Almost every area of activity in the working environment is bounded by processes.

Some business/management examples are:

- Planning
- Coaching
- Recruiting
- Managing/appraising performance

The most basic or general action-based process that is widely adapted is:

Although there are many problem-solving models about, most commentators agree that there are certain basic processes that need to be ordered in some kind of sequence. These include:

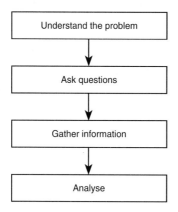

The model we propose is not a detailed algorithm that can be rigidly applied step by step, but a general description of the basic processes in order, that encompasses most of the associated sub-processes.

The model, if used properly, will assist you to tackle even the most intractable problems.

The 4A model of problem-solving

There are many models of the problem-solving process to be found. Some are more detailed and prescriptive than others. However, most of them can be interpreted as having four basic stages. These four stages are incorporated into the 4A model.

Setting the Agenda Getting a feel for the territory surrounding the problem, which culminates in a detailed statement of the problem.

Audit The process of clarifying the major elements and dimensions of the problem – acquiring information, defining the plan of attack.

Analysis The evaluation stage, sometimes involving scientific processes of testing and verification, sometimes involving breaking down (analysis), and sometimes involving a putting back together of the parts (synthesis).

Action The enabling stage where we formulate a plan of action to complete the cycle.

Although each stage is pushed along by the asking of pertinent questions in a systematic way, different kinds of thinking are required at each of the stages. There are convergent and divergent influences working at each of these stages, as illustrated in the diagram.

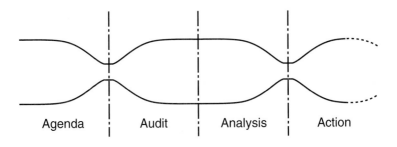

| Agenda | Audit | Analysis | Action |

Agenda

At the Agenda stage, we are scanning for information, which means looking inward towards the problem. But the purpose of this stage is to focus in on a detailed definition of the problem, a set of criteria, objectives or outcomes, which will enable us to judge whether we have adequately solved the problem. Thus it is basically a convergent process.

The key components and processes at this stage are:

- Acquaintance
- Focus
- Definition of problem
- Convergence
- Clarification
- Scanning
- Categorisation

In PS-type problems, the defined outcome will be to identify, test and verify the cause of the problem. For these problems, we know only too well that we have a problem, as some malfunction presents itself to us. This is usually a deterioration in circumstances, and can be quite noticeable. However, it is not always easy in incrementally deteriorating circumstances to know when to acknowledge that there is a problem.

In PF-type problems, or design-led problems, the Agenda stage is used to set criteria for a successful outcome.

However, it is not always easy to define a problem. If a customer complains, it might be easy to define the attitude of the customer as the problem. You might then be able to try (and you might be successful) in placating him or her. However, if the real cause of their dissatisfaction is not investigated and rectified, the problem will only recur.

When defining a problem you need to ask:

If I fix this (find the cause, etc.), will the problem situation be rectified?

If not, you need to move back a step, or move to the next logical level.

Faced with such circumstances, the natural inclinations of many people leads them to two fundamental mistakes. Take the example of someone faced with having to 'solve' the problem of an ailing company which is making losses.

The first mistake people make is that they often jump straight to decision-making. In this case, this would lead them, for instance, to sack the managing director, or move the head office.

Decisions taken without the prior problem analysis are much less likely to be right, or to stick, because they are taken in ignorance of the real problems.

Secondly, when looking for a definition of the problem, most people tend to pitch it at the wrong level.

Typical first reactions might be that the company has a 'motivation' problem, for instance. It is important to tackle a problem at the highest logical level. In this case the highest level problem is that the company is making losses. The cause of this needs to be established before tackling the lower level problems like motivation. (This is not to say that motivation is not important – just that solving it would not help, if the company continues to make losses.)

To summarise, then, the major outcomes from the Agenda stage are *acquaintance* with the problem, and a *definition* of it.

Audit
At Audit we are opening out to seek information, to make a map of the problem space, to generate patterns, to intuit cause and effect, to spot connections. It is equivalent to playing with the pieces of a jigsaw. Thus it is a divergent phase.

The key components and processes are:

- Understanding what's going on
- Conceptualisation
- Description of the problem space
- Ideation and model building
- Cause and effect

- Plan of attack
- Making connections, identifying patterns
- Collecting information
- Divergence

The major outcomes of the Audit stage are a *model of the problem*, and a *plan of attack* for its solution.

Analysis
At Analysis we are putting the pieces back together again. We have identified possible causes and collected information. Now we test our ideas. We are converging on a 'solution' to the problem.

This stage is often highly detailed and involves the use of systematic, often quantitative tools.

The key components and processes are:

- Convergence
- Testing and checking out
- Logic
- Collecting information

The major outcome of the Analysis stage involves confirmation of guesses and hunches, validation of our cause–effect models, all leading to a *solution*.

Action
At the Action stage we may be involved in a number of processes. The results of the previous stage may specify the requirements of this stage in quite a detailed way (i.e. they may be convergent).

Alternatively, it may put us into a decision-making process, which will again require us to 'open out'. In other words, this may be a convergent or a divergent phase, depending on the nature of the problem and the outcomes of the analysis phase.

However, the requirements here follow automatically from the previous stages, and are usually self-evident.

The components and processes include:

- Decision-making
- Implementation
- Operations
- Evaluation

The major outcome here is obviously *completion*.

Summary

For us to be successful problem-solvers at work, we need to have a structured, systematic and sequential approach. Today we have looked at the 'science' of problem-solving, its origins and its application to business contexts.

We have explored the 4A model for problem-solving and identified its four major stages:

- **A**genda – defining the problem
- **A**udit – clarifying and building models of the cause–effect processes
- **A**nalysis – logical examination and testing of the processes involved
- **A**ction – enabling final completion

Now that we have examined the processes behind problem-solving, we will go on tomorrow to look at the tools and techniques for successful problem-solving.

The tools of the trade

Each problem is in some ways unique, and different problems offer different challenges.

Over the years many people have invented, adapted or used a variety of tools and techniques that can be used with different kinds of problems, and at certain stages of the problem-solving process.

These tools and techniques can be classified into three types:

1 Tools for organising information and concepts
2 Process-based tools
3 Quantitative tools

Organising information and concepts

One of the first tasks that faces us when we tackle a problem is the need to collect information. This need exists at each stage of the problem-solving process, but is particularly acute at the first two stages: Agenda and Audit.

At the early, more open-ended or divergent stages of the problem-solving process, this can be difficult because a 'model' of the problem space may not exist, and there may be considerable fuzziness about the information available and the information required.

Acquiring information usually involves some kind of structured approach, and this will be dependent on the context of the problem.

Some of the various ways of acquiring information include:

- Face-to-face interview or discussion
- Research – via reference sources, databases or libraries
- Surveys – using questionnaires, or other structured means

The other important requirement at this stage is for the information to be organised or structured. This may involve any of a number of processes. These might include:

- Gaining clarity by grasping the totality of the information
- Building a model of the problem space
- Cutting through the mass of information to get to the key ideas or priorities

A number of techniques can be used to achieve these. However, amongst the difficulties that face the problem-solver are:

- Large quantities of information
- Complexity of information
- Conceptual/abstract nature of ideas/information involved

For many people it can be difficult to juggle with large amounts of complex information or concepts, or, in other words, to map the information or concept space that surrounds the problem.

We know from psychology that the average person can process about seven bits or chunks of information at a time. Yet the information space surrounding many complex problems takes us well over the seven limit. We therefore need strategies to sort, organise and manage large amounts of information or concepts.

One of the simplest ways to begin to do this is to make a list. This simple approach is very underused, yet it can be a surprisingly effective way of clearing the fog.

Lists can be structured according to specific purposes. For instance, in open-ended or future-oriented business contexts, a **SWOT** analysis can be a good way of structuring thoughts on a potential problem. To do this you just list the **S**trengths, **W**eaknesses, **O**pportunities and **T**hreats. This then provides the raw material for further analysis.

We know that many people who are successful at capturing and organising large information spaces in their head use visual strategies to do so. Such strategies can be easily learned and adapted for use in problem-solving.

Mind mapping
The first and easiest technique is the mind map, or visual 'brain dump'. It involves taking the central theme, topic or idea and adding keyword 'legs' to the spider. Each 'leg' can again be subdivided, until a space has been exhausted. Lines can be added to show relationships or connections and they can be enhanced by visual effects such as colour, size and the use of images.

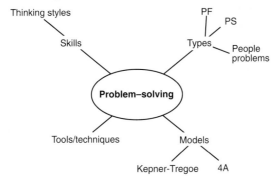

Not only does the map capture the information, it can also imply hierarchy or structure. In fact, an initial mind map (which often looks like a plate of spaghetti) can be given a second pass to add structure and coherence, as in the examples which follow in the structure diagram section.

Mind maps can be used for all sorts of purposes: taking notes when reading; increasing comprehension; aiding memory; planning reports; analysing processes.

A variation is called a Fishbone Diagram or Ishikawa Diagram. They are used for 'quick and dirty' problem-solving in front-line situations. They are a simple way of brainstorming possible causes of a problem.

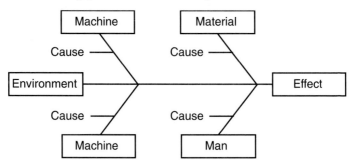

Structure diagrams
There are many ways to add structure to a map of an information or concept space.

The structure can be ordered linearly:

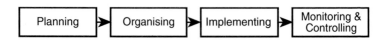

Or there can be a multi-linear or hierarchical structure:

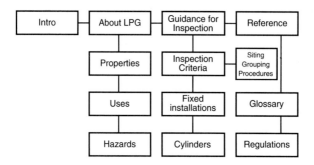

Process-based tools

Information maps can be adapted to illustrate processes. Perhaps the simplest way to do this is to add a time line.

This particular version, called a Gantt Chart, is very useful for project planning purposes.

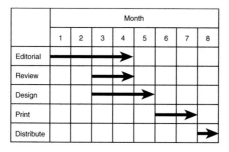

It is constructed by breaking a project down into its constituent tasks. These are then listed in the left-hand column. The start time and duration of each activity or task is indicated by an arrow on the time line. Some of these can overlap, but some need to be sequential (for instance, you can't print a book until it is written and designed).

A simple process can be shown in a flow diagram.

Increasingly, data flow diagrams (DFDs) are used to define relationships within systems. They are constructed to show the main types of operation in a system – input, processing and output.

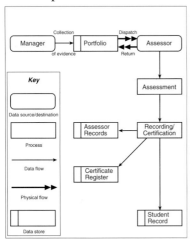

This DFD illustrates the examination process for the Certificate in Management Studies programme.

Quantitative tools

Numerical or quantitative information may be collected at any stage of a problem-solving process. It should follow on naturally from the basic questions or descriptions of a situation (described more fully tomorrow). These relate to the dimensions of:

- Identity – What?
- Location – Where?
- Timing – When? (How often?)
- Magnitude – How much? How many?

This information can be collected, organised and illustrated by a variety of means. These include bar charts and pie charts, which are available on most good spreadsheets.

Most people will be familiar with these simple techniques,
but there are two others you may not be so familiar with,
but which have many applications in problem-solving
situations.

Pareto analysis
Pareto analysis is used to prioritise problems for solution or
to isolate the most important factors in a problem.

The analysis is based on the Pareto Principle or 80:20 rule:

e.g.   80% of sales came from 20% of customers

80% of stock value is in 20% of the parts

Consider an example. The steps involved are:

1 Determine ideas to be investigated (possibly by
   brainstorming).
2 Collect appropriate numerical data.

This is shown below for mistakes arising in typed standard
letters from an insurance company.

Error/factor			Month 1996		
	Jan	Feb	Mar	Apr	Total
Wrong name/address	8	6	12	9	35
Wrong title/appellation	22	17	18	27	84
Typing/spelling	14	8	12	10	44
Wrong standard letter	5	8	3	5	21
Wrong format	3	6	1	2	12
Other	3	0	3	4	10

3 Draw up a frequency table.

This table highlights the frequency for each category as well as the relative frequency and the cumulative frequency (by adding up the frequencies as you go along). Notice that the categories are placed in rank order – biggest first.

Error	Frequency	Relative %	Cumulative Frequency	Cumulative %
Wrong title	84	40.8	84	40.8
Typing	44	21.4	128	62.1
Wrong name/ address	35	17.0	163	79.1
Wrong letter	21	10.2	184	89.3
Wrong format	12	5.8	196	95.1
Other	10	4.8	206	100

Notice that the first three categories account for 80% of the errors. This can be seen even more clearly if we construct a Pareto diagram.

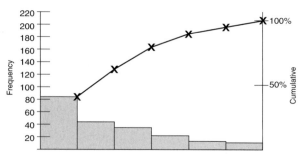

We plot bars for the frequencies and crosses for the cumulative frequencies.

The analysis identifies the major causes of errors, and enables us to begin to address them, either by investigating their cause or by taking corrective action.

Thus the diagram identifies the factors that have most impact on a problem, and hence directs our efforts to the most important areas.

Scatter diagrams
This is a graphic method for determining cause and effect relationships by analysing patterns.

Where information suggests connection between two factors in a problem, the pattern in a scatter diagram indicates if there is a relationship.

For instance we might suspect that the number of incoming calls to a telephone answering service is related to the time of day. To find out, we would collect information relating the two variables and plot them on axes. The line of best fit should be drawn.

The relationship between the variables may not always be indicated by a straight line, but may be as shown in the diagrams.

Obviously, the closer the points cluster to the line, the stronger the correlation between the variables.

Hybrid techniques
Every problem is unique, and not all problems fit neatly into categories. This can sometimes make it difficult to fit the techniques outlined here to some problems. Sometimes it is

necessary to invent your own techniques, or adapt, to solve a particular problem.

Take the traffic light problem mentioned on Sunday.

The PF-type problem is to analyse and classify the relationships when the traffic lights are set in certain ways. A visual/tabular technique is a good way to do this. So we can represent each setting of the lights with a table.

↑ means straight on in that direction
← means turn left in that direciton
→ means turn right in that direction

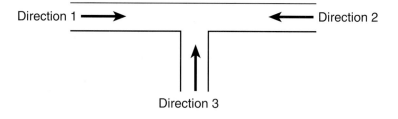

	Direction 1 ↑ →		Direction 2 ↑ ←		Direction 3 ← →	
Setting 1	✓	✗	✓	✓	✗	✗
Setting 2	✓	✓	✗	✗	✓	✗
Setting 3	✗	✗	✗	✓	✓	✓

Once we understand the nature of the settings we can look at the order in which the settings will rotate.

We can also look at the timings, and these will be dictated by a look at the traffic volumes. From this start, it will be fairly easy to compare traffic volumes at any time of day with the potential traffic flow allowed by the settings and the phasing.

This problem, like many others, shows that it is difficult to 'look up' the relevant technique in a text book. Sometimes the imagination and creativity in problem-solving are in the ability to invent an appropriate technique to make sense of the information in front of you.

The tools outlined in this chapter should help you to collect, structure, organise and analyse information in many different ways, depending on the nature of the problem. Some may have more use at different stages of the problem-solving model. For instance, the SWOT analysis is well suited to scanning at the agenda stage of the problem.

Ishikawa diagrams and mind maps are well suited to the divergent thinking required at the audit phase.

Pareto analysis and scatter diagrams are more likely to figure at the analysis phase of the process.

However you should not be limited by these suggestions as all problems are unique, and you should choose the tools appropriate to your needs – whatever stage you are at.

Summary

Each problem is unique and the tools and techniques used should relate to the particular requirements of the specific problem and the phase of the problem you are at.

Today we have identified and explored the three main categories of tools and techniques for problem-solving:

1 Organising information and concepts
2 Process-based structures
3 Quantitative tools

Tomorrow we will go on to examine one particular approach to the analysis and solution of problems.

The Kepner–Tregoe approach

We will set out here the problem analysis technique developed and used by Charles Kepner and Ben Tregoe.

We will look at:

- The rational management approach
- The problem analysis process
- Uses of problem analysis

The rational management approach

Kepner and Tregoe were among the first to set out a systematic approach to the analysis of cause–effect processes in the business domain. They studied the thinking processes of successful managers, and discovered that four basic patterns of thinking were adopted.

These were ordered in the following way:

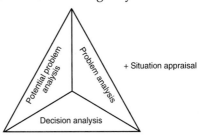

Each one is associated with a particular kind of thinking and an associated set of questions.

What's going on? This is associated with situation review.

Why did this happen? This is associated with the analysis of cause and effect, and gives rise to the processes of problem analysis.

What should we do? This is about the evaluation of possible courses of action, and is called decision analysis.

What lies ahead? This is future-oriented and is about anticipating potential problems and contingency planning for them.

They were among the first to make a clear distinction between problem-solving and decision-making. We have not adopted their very clear distinction between the two. Our definition and approach to problems and problem-solving incorporates elements of situation review and potential problem analysis, as well as problem analysis.

However, their technique for solving problems in situations where there is a defined and clear deviation from a norm or expectation, and where the cause is unknown, is very rigorous and very effective.

Its target is the identification of unknown causes of dysfunction in a system, and, in problems where that is required, this is the most systematic and effective of techniques.

Kepner and Tregoe have developed and used their technique over many years. As well as teaching the processes, they have tackled problems for many large organisations, including NASA and the US military.

Our major concern here is with the problem analysis, so let us set out the Kepner–Tregoe process for the analysis of problems.

Problem analysis

As we have said, this process is rigorous and systematic. Some problems can be dealt with 'on the run' and can be solved or fixed with a little knowledge or inspiration. Others are more major, and need full analysis. In the case of such major problems, guesswork is not good enough. There may be too much at stake, and guesses or hunches may not be adequate.

This process should be applied in quite strict circumstances. This is when:

There is a deviation from a norm or expectation, with an unknown cause.

The process, therefore, is the analysis of cause and effect, and is successfully concluded when the cause has been identified, tested and verified.

The whole process is as follows:

1 Definition of a problem
2 Description of the problem

3 Collection of information and identification of possible causes
4 Testing for probable causes
5 Verification of true cause

1 Definition of problem
Problems can arise in two basic ways.

A typical deviation:

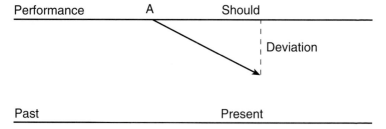

This situation arises where performance has been satisfactory, and for some reason has deteriorated, or dropped off. Clearly, what happens at point A is going to be significant, because what has changed there will be part of the causal chain.

A day one problem:

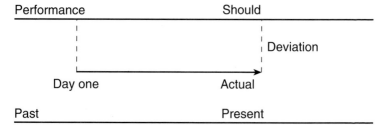

In this case some condition for proper functioning has never been there. Things have not been right since the beginning.

In defining a problem, it is important to distinguish between symptoms and effects. For instance:

- Symptom: poor attitude at work, tiredness
- Cause: illness
- Effect: loss of productivity and effectiveness

In problem analysis what we need to identify is the effect – the performance deviation for which we need to identify the cause.

Sometimes we need to backtrack from an apparent statement if the stated deviation has a known cause. We need to ask the question:

Does this effect have a known cause?

If the answer is 'yes', then we backtrack to the next level, until we find a problem statement that has no identifiable cause.

2 *Problem description*
It is in this area that Kepner and Tregoe have brought a detailed and scientific approach to the description of problems. They have used a set of parameters or dimensions of description that, when used properly, provide a comprehensive description of a problem.

They have been adapted from the ideas of Isaac Newton, who used them for describing the world in scientific terms.

The four dimensions are:

- **Identity**
- **Location**
- **Timing**
- **Magnitude**

The problem is then described in some detail, by the use of a set of questions for each dimension.

- **Identity**
  - What unit/object is the problem?
  - What exactly is the problem or deviation?
- **Location**
  - Where is it (geographically)?
  - Where on the unit/object?
- **Timing**
  - When was it first observed?
  - When does it happen?
  - How often does it happen?

- **Magnitude**
  - To what extent?
  - How much...?
  - How many...?

These questions are really no more than common sense, and would be used in many circumstances by 'natural' problem-solvers.

If you have a child that is ill, you would be asking the same set of questions:

- What is wrong with you?
- Where is the pain?
- When did it start?
- How often do you get it?
- How bad is it?
- Is it getting better or worse?

The main difference here is that the questioning is comprehensive and systematic. The richer and more complete you can make the description, the more likely you are to uncover the clue that will reveal the cause of the problem.

The description itself is put into a table, like the one shown below.

Problem specification matrix			
	Description	**Comparison**	**Differences**
Identity			
Location			
Timing			
Magnitude			

Logical comparison This next stage is unique to this process, and the one that makes it so efficient. What we describe here are the comparative data, on the basis of:

What is not a problem, but could be?

This is a well-established scientific approach, but has not been generally applied to the business context.

Imagine the scientific testing of a new drug. Scientists will use a control group, who do not receive the drug. Why is this? What information can this group give about the performance of the drug with the chosen sample of users?

The answer is that it can give comparative data, which is vital in cause and effect analysis.

If the two groups are, to all intents and purposes, exactly the same, then any differences throughout the trial can be ascribed to the drug itself. In other words, they are used to isolate the effects of the drug on a comparative basis.

If two identical pot plants are placed in a house, and one thrives while the other does not, we can reasonably conclude that something is different about them, and that this difference accounts for their respective fortunes – is it the sunlight, the temperature, the humidity?

The 'is not, but could be' data provide a basis for logical comparison.

The comparative data is then added to the matrix (see page 51).

3 Identification of possible causes

With the comparative data, we can now begin to identify what the distinctions might be. These will enable us to ask the most important question:

Why might these be different?

These differences or distinctions are set out in a separate column of the table (see page 51).

We are now close to identifying potential causal mechanisms.

Having identified what is different about 'the problem' and 'not the problem', we can start to provide explanations as to why this might be. Of course, at each stage in the process it is necessary to go and find information to describe and model the problem and the situation further.

Somewhere in this list lies the solution to the problem – the difference that makes a difference. This is as long as the original description is comprehensive enough.

If little of significance is emerging from this analysis, another pass through the description and logical comparison is required.

Eventually, though, we will have enough information here, and we will be able to identify which of these factors can account for the change.

It is important to make a statement of all possible causes, for further testing. At this stage, the ideas we have are just guesses. They now need to be tested.

4 *Testing for causes*
For each possible cause we now need to ask:

If this is the cause, does it explain all of the effects?

In other words, we identify not just the possible cause, but what the mechanism might be.

This testing phase is a logical 'if-then' process. It is based on the assumption that things will stay the same unless some part of the system changes. The possible cause analysis gives us ideas as to what changes may be taking place. The testing allows us to work out how any particular change may produce the effects noted in the description.

5 *Verification*
Once we feel that we have identified the mechanism, and we have tested it, we can verify it. This involves reversing the changes that have taken place to see if the problem is eliminated.

If we have identified an offending component, when we replace it, the problem should cease.

If we have identified that somebody has been applying an incorrect procedure in certain circumstances, when the correct procedure is applied this should eliminate the problem.

Uses of problem analysis

This process is very efficient, and has been tried and tested in the most complex and demanding circumstances. However, it can be a juggernaut. A problem might need to be quite substantial or important to justify the time spent on a full analysis.

The other alternative is to use a 'quick and dirty' approach to a problem. This would involve a problem description (which may perhaps require a brainstorm), which then focuses clearly on one or other of the dimensions.

For instance, sometimes it is clear quite early on that time is the key dimension, that the time description has very clear and significant features, and that this can quickly be pursued, to the exclusion of the rest of the full analysis.

This is perfectly adequate if it yields up the required causes, and if they check out through the test and verification stages.

It may also be that this approach looks slightly 'odd' or unfamiliar. If this is the case it is probably because we are unused to being so systematic. For many of us, our natural tendency is to work on guesses and hunches. The value of this approach is precisely because it eliminates the guesswork.

I can only suggest that you become familiar with the approach by using it on a (fairly modest) problem from your own experience. This will enable you to see how it works in practice, and to get used to the processes involved.

Summary

Problem analysis is a process that involves the systematic tracking down of unknown causes in situations where there is a deviation form a norm or expectation. Today we have looked at the stages involved in that process:

1 Definition of deviation
2 Description of problem
3 Identification of possible causes
4 Testing
5 Verification

Tomorrow we go on to look at people problems and possible approaches for solving problems that involve people.

People and problems

People problems can be amongst the most intractable and difficult type of problems to deal with. If business-related problems have more variables and unknowns than scientific or mathematical problems, then people problems are even more difficult to pin down.

Today, we will consider:

- People problems
- Managing change
- Solving problems in groups
- Team roles

People problems

People problems tend to arise from one of the following reasons:

- Lack of knowledge or information
- Lack of skill
- Attitude or motivation

Knowledge
Knowledge problems tend to arise when people do not know or understand what it is they are supposed to do. This may be in relation to systems, procedures or the use of equipment. In these cases the symptoms tend to show up as a system or equipment problem, and these will be tackled using the methods and techniques set out in previous days.

When any failure has taken place, it is always worth checking for the possibility of human error. Of course, things can go wrong just simply because people have made mistakes.

The difference between a mistake and a lack of knowledge or understanding can only be identified by thorough checking – again the skill is in asking questions and seeking information in a sensitive manner.

Once such problems have been identified, they are usually the easiest to rectify – it is simply a matter of providing people with the appropriate opportunity to develop the knowledge and understanding, and then confirming that they have it.

An example would be a cleaner on a cleaning schedule. Do they know the health and safety procedures associated with the materials they use, or the equipment they clean? They might not know, for instance, why two substances should not be mixed together.

It is a question of communication. Just because a list says use substance X followed by substance Y, you should not assume that people understand why.

Skill

Skill problems can be more difficult to deal with for a number of reasons. First, when something goes wrong, it is not always obvious that the cause is related to a lack of skill. As with knowledge problems, these need careful diagnosis and checking.

We often do not know explicitly what skills are required to perform a particular job. Neither do we often know what skills staff have without some kind of systematic audit or training needs analysis.

Skill and knowledge problems can be diagnosed by examining performance.

People and performance problems often fall in between the extremes we set out on Sunday:

Broken ◄─────────────────────────────► Fixed

In many working contexts, things are rarely perfect, and an accumulation of minor errors or problems is almost inevitable.

There are many tools appropriate to the audit phase that can be used here to diagnose problems. Major problem areas can be identified by Pareto analysis.

However, there is no substitute for talking to people to find out what they are doing – or not doing. But there needs to be a standard; you need to know what they are supposed to be able to do, and so do they.

Once this is available, it is then possible to match the skills to the requirements. This is a training needs analysis.

Once this diagnosis has been done, appropriate methods should be identified to meet needs.

These can include a wide range of options:

- On-the-job training
- Work shadowing
- Coaching
- Work-based tasks or projects
- Short courses

Attitude and motivation
A large number of problems that occur at work are ascribed to attitude or motivational issues.

It is important to recognise that this is very difficult territory and to deal with it needs much more than the analytic skills and processes set out in this book. It needs a very high level of interpersonal skills from those who have to intervene to 'solve' such problems.

Another aspect is that cause and effect relationships are much more difficult to discern in such problems. This is because poor attitude or morale may be both the cause of problems and the symptom of them. Another complication is that the attitude and performance of any one individual is intimately tied up with that of other members of the team and with the culture of the whole organisation.

In dealing with a problem at the level of the individual, you should bear in mind the culture, expectations and ways of doing things that exist in the group or team. To some extent, they will influence the habits and attitudes of the individual.

Sometimes we identify people problems in the general rather than the specific way. Nothing major has gone wrong, but we are aware that things are just not right. In these cases, the most important skill is that of listening.

Listening
Listening is probably the most important channel we have for obtaining information. Yet it can be a surprisingly inefficient means of getting quality information. When it comes to problems of attitude and motivation, there is very little alternative.

In order to increase the efficiency of your listening capability, you should pay attention to the basic rules of active listening:

- Let the other person do the talking
- Demonstrate attention by eye contact and body language
- Acknowledge what they have said
- Ask 'what' and 'why' questions to elicit information

But what do we do when we do listen? We often have a tendency to:

- Interpret too early
- Make assumptions too early
- Make decisions too early

In other words, we often wade in and solve problems before we have a good understanding of what is going on.

In people problems we should learn to gather information first, and only then seek appropriate action. That action should also be owned by the individual involved. We do not tend to trust as much as we should, and we do not often give people the credit for sorting out their own problems.

The skills of a mentor or facilitator are appropriate here. We should learn to assist people by questioning in order to identify or diagnose the problem, identify possible solutions and resource and assist them in fulfilling those solutions.

People themselves are often best placed to understand and solve their own problems, if we give them respect, space and assistance in dealing with them.

Finally, listening has a further benefit in that it helps to give the message that we are interested in the opinions of the other person. Such involvement, control and consultation are known to increase motivation.

Managing change

Change in organisations brings with it many problems. It is important to recognise that change is difficult and threatening for people. It is all too easy (and quite common) for organisations to focus on the task or the technical aspects of proposed changes and ignore the people dimension.

So when problems do occur, the causes and the issues can be difficult to untangle.

We don't have space here to give a full coverage of the subject of managing change, but we can suggest one useful technique for analysing potential problems in change environments.

This is called Force Field Analysis, and stems from the work of Kurt Lewin.

In Force Field Analysis, we look at the potential change or initiative, and isolate two sets of forces.

Driving forces These are the forces tending to produce movement towards the goal.

Restraining forces These are the forces or barriers tending to resist the change.

These forces should be stated in as much specific detail as possible. They are then listed on a table like the one below.

Driving forces	Restraining forces	Actions to take

This then enables an analysis to take place about how to increase driving forces and decrease restraining forces, where there is leverage on the system and linkage between components.

It is a simple tool, but it does enable complicated situations to be clarified, and it does enable cause–effect processes to be analysed.

Solving problems in groups

It is appropriate in this people section to discuss the role of groups in relation to problem-solving. This is not so much about solving group or team problems, but about using groups to solve problems.

Meetings

Group discussions and meetings are a very common way of dealing with problems. However, like many people, you have probably had the experience of unproductive meetings, or meetings where time is wasted and little gets done.

A few guidelines should help to impose discipline on a meeting and so aid effectiveness.

Meeting guidelines:

- Make sure the right people are present
- Prepare properly and present information clearly
- Define and communicate the purposes of the meeting with an agenda, and reinforce it at the beginning of the meeting
- Invite and acknowledge contributions from all involved
- Encourage a productive style of leadership
- Minimise conflict and unhelpful digressions
- Record decisions and allocate responsibilities

Brainstorming

Brainstorming is probably one of the most powerful of all problem-solving tools. Its purpose is to generate a large amount of ideas from a group of people.

It works on the principle of synergy – that is, that the group can generate more than the sum of the individuals. This is because each idea produces further ideas that can be built upon.

The first task in a brainstorm is to generate ideas about the defined topic in hand.

Brainstorming guidelines:

- Take turns in offering ideas
- The more ideas the better
- Record ideas as they are generated
- All ideas should be valued, therefore...
- No criticism or evaluation at this stage

Only when a good stock of ideas has been generated does the group turn to evaluating ideas. Ideas can be re-ordered, connections made, and patterns built up.

The use of visual aids can assist in this process enormously. Flipcharts are commonly used. Post-it™ notes are also useful, as they can be moved into groups or hierarchies.

Team roles

For teams to be effective they need a balance of skills and attributes that each of the members can contribute to the whole. People are selected for their role in a team or group on the basis of some functional or technical expertise.

However, research has also confirmed that individuals adopt a team role, and different team roles contribute different things.

R.M. Belbin, *Team Roles at Work* (Heinemann, Oxford, 1993), has identified the following team roles that people adopt:

Plants Creative innovators. Good at generating new ideas, but these may often be impractical. Tend to be loners, and need praise.

Resource investigators Good communicators and negotiators. Good at developing ideas. Tend to be extrovert, enthusiastic and relaxed.

Monitor evaluators Good at analysing and evaluating. Tend to be thoughtful, cautious, but can be over-critical.

Co-ordinators Good leaders who develop people and ideas. They tend to be mature and confident.

Shapers Single-minded challengers who have a bias for action. Tend to be driven and competitive.

Implementors Hard-working and efficient pragmatists. Tend to be reliable and disciplined.

Teamworkers Flexible, adaptable, sociable. Tend to avoid conflict and seek cooperation.

Completer finishers Detailed, accurate, setting high standards, they see the job through. They tend to be introverted and intolerant of sloppiness.

Specialists Have professional standards in a specific technical skill. Tend to be dedicated and proud individuals.

Of course, not everyone fits neatly into one of these roles. But if you think of a team or group that you are familiar with, you may be able to identify behaviours that relate to the roles described above.

What does this tell us about teams? Successful teams have a balance of roles within them. Knowing about team role behaviour should enable you to value the different contributions of people to teams you work with.

Knowledge of team roles should also help to allocate work and responsibilities on a more 'horses for courses' basis.

Summary

Today we have seen how people problems can arise and how they can be among the most difficult to handle. They can arise through:

- Lack of knowledge or information
- Lack of skill
- Problems of attitude and motivation

We have looked at how change can further complicate people problems and how solutions can be found through group and team work.

Tomorrow we will look at developing the skills that will make you a successful problem-solver.

Skills of problem-solving

We have examined in some detail the processes involved in problem-solving and the tools and techniques that are associated with these processes. But these would be valueless without problem-solvers who have the repertoire of skills to make them work. As we have said, problem-solving is more than the mere application of a set of rules. Their successful application requires the use of a wide range of skills and attributes. It is to these that we turn today.

We will consider:

- Knowledge and attitude
- Heuristic skills
- Creativity

Knowledge and attitude

Perhaps one of the easiest ways to think of the range of skills and attributes is to view them as a triad, as shown in the diagram.

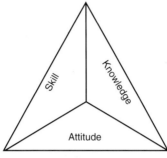

Knowledge

The point has already been made that problem-solving usually takes place in the context of some knowledge base. We quoted the example of the car mechanic, who seems to have 'radar' because of his knowledge of mechanics and an in-depth awareness of the relationships between the parts.

Good problem-solving needs to be embedded in an experience base. The reason for this is that much problem-solving is about identifying and untangling cause and effect patterns. This can obviously be better done where some of these patterns and connections already exist.

Most of us have some substantial knowledge base, whether it be in relation to some technical field or some particular business context. This should give a good platform for solving problems in that particular area.

It should be noted, however, that this can also, in certain circumstances, be a disadvantage. This is because we often have tramlines or rigid or limited preconceptions of cause and effect chains. These can sometimes inhibit open-mindedness, and prevent us from being objective about the evidence in front of us. In fact, it can even prevent us from pursuing a course that a more objective observer can suggest.

You may well have heard of examples similar to the experience of the scientist, who was trying to describe some intractable technical problem to his grandmother, only for her to make exactly the right suggestion. The scientist had not been able to see the simple solution, precisely because he was too close to the problem.

But all in all, as long as we are open-minded, a sound knowledge base is an advantage, and if you don't have it in relation to a particular problem, it is wise to pick the brains of someone who has.

Attitude

It is easy and tempting to focus on skills as the only important prerequisite for the ability to solve problems. But to exclude the importance of attitude would be a mistake.

Because solving problems is not easy, there are certain qualities that help us to put our skills to good and successful use. These include:

- Determination
- Tolerance of detail
- Open-mindedness
- Ability to cope with dead ends, being stuck
- Initiative
- Focus and single-mindedness
- The need to know

Embedded in a number of these attributes is the ability to stick with a task and see it through to the end. The 'butterfly' approach does not go a long way to solving problems.

Heuristic skills

As we have said, the purely mechanical application of any sequence or process is not enough in itself to enable problems to be solved. It is required to develop and apply a wide range of skills at various stages of the sequence in order to progress and be successful.

These skills fall into a number of categories:

- Information processing
- Analytic or process skills
- The ability to monitor progress
- Asking quality questions

Information processing
At the centre of the business of solving problems is the ability to process information. This involves a number of distinct processes.

1 Obtaining quality information

This involves:

- Constantly monitoring, scanning and checking the internal and external environment
- Seeking up-to-date and relevant information

- Checking information for validity and reliability
- Using all available sources and channels of information

2 Organising information

This involves:

- Re-ordering and simplifying the information available
- Weeding out unnecessary information or 'noise'
- Structuring or ordering information so it is usable

3 Evaluating information

This involves:

- Understanding the significance of the information
- Being able to draw appropriate conclusions

Analytic or process skills
Analytic skills are highly valued in many areas of working life – and no less so in the domain of problem-solving. They involve the ability to manipulate ideas and concepts, and to put ideas together into logical chains of reasoning.

Among the separate processes involved are:

Analysis and synthesis These involve decomposing a problem into components to separate out the parts, and recombining or 'putting the parts of the jigsaw back together again'.

Deductive and inductive reasoning The former involves using a set of statements or premises and drawing legitimate conclusions from them. Inductive reasoning, by contrast, involves taking specific examples and generalising from the few to the many. It is more of a 'trial and error' process.

Modelling processes and cause and effect chains This is the flexibility to play with ideas and a tolerance of ambiguity and complexity. It is the ability to work in semi-structured information spaces or concept spaces. It involves the ability to model a process or concept space in the mind, in order to understand what is going on and why (the cause and effect chains), and to manipulate that model according to information received. To do this involves an innate sense of pattern, symmetry and connectivity, by being able to relate facts and ideas to some known database.

There are also a whole range of subskills that it is useful to call upon – the ability to:

- Make analogies with known problems and situations
- Test hunches and guesses
- Take a small part of the problem, or a simpler problem
- Develop strategies or plans of attack

Monitoring progress
Research shows that effective problem-solvers are also able to monitor their own progress through the solution of a problem. They do this by always keeping an eye on the rate of progress.

Thus, good problem-solvers are those who ask questions like:

How am I doing?
Am I making progress?
Is this getting us anywhere?
Is this line of enquiry worth pursuing?
What else is worth trying?

The reason why this is effective is that it prevents the waste of time on blind alleys and strategies that lead nowhere. By checking the effectiveness of an approach or strategy you can constantly adjust, and focus energy and effort where progress is being made.

Questions
This leads us on naturally to the importance of questions. Most analytic systems are built around the systematic asking of judicious questions. Often these questions can

seem simple, or even trivial. Yet it is the asking and answering of simple questions that is the engine or driving force of most structured analytic procedures.

The questions that are used will obviously relate to the specific problem in hand, and to the stage of the problem-solving process that you are at.

At Agenda stage, typical questions are:

What is this problem about?
How will I know if I have solved the problem?

At the Audit stage:

How does the information I have relate to the unknown?
Have I seen a problem like this before?
What factors are involved?
How does this work?

At the Analysis stage:

In what way is this component related to this component?

If I do this... what will happen?
How can I be sure?
Does this explain the known facts or effects?

At the Action stage:

What comes next?
What will complete the process?

We can illustrate how questions are used to help solve a problem by looking at an example.

The problem is to find a way to connect A to a, B to b and C to c.

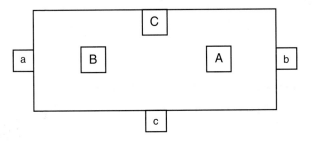

The Agenda stage of this problem is quite easy, because the problem is clearly stated, and it is quite bounded and unambiguous.

At the Audit stage, what we need to do is to get familiar with the problem space.

So the first question is:

Can I do something easy?

You will notice that it is easy to connect C to c. Sometimes it is a good strategy to go for the line of least resistance and see what happens. In this case, what happens is that it seems to make the problem impossible.

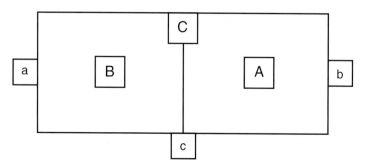

If that doesn't work, the next strategy is to ask:

What else can I try?

Notice that here we are just 'playing' with the problem – trying to get a feel for the important components and relationships.

The next strategy to try is to connect B to b and A to a. We need to put a 'wave' in, in order to do this. We do it, not because we know it is the solution, but because it is something worth trying. It is an important problem-solving strategy to have the flexibility to try things on the basis of 'let's see what happens'.

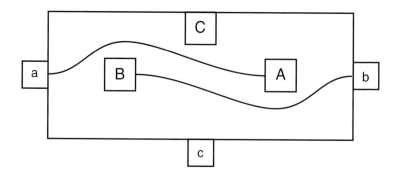

Does this help?

We didn't know it when we tried it, but this is a crucial stage. By being willing to try things out (and not demanding the answer complete and neat the first time), by being able to be playful, tolerant of uncertainty and not being able to see the destination, we have arrived at a situation from where the solution is possible. You may be able to see it from here.

If you don't – as always – start asking questions:

Is it possible to join C to c from here? (If you don't know – try it.)

What do I need in order for it to be possible?

What other tack could I try...?

and so on. The whole process is driven by questions and the willingness to try things out.

An exposition of how a mathematician might solve the problem is given in the introduction to G. Polya's *How To Solve It* by I. Stewart, Penguin, 1990.

Creativity

Creativity is such a difficult concept to discuss because we all know what we think we mean by it – but we all mean different things!

Creativity exists in so many forms and in so many areas of human life and achievement, and that makes it hard to pin down. What is certain is that we all have a great, and often untapped or underused potential for creativity. Most of us describe as creative only a fraction of those skills and capacities that should be considered as such.

In terms of problem-solving, there are a number of scales which we can use to talk about the notion of creativity.

The first is the *convergent–divergent* scale. This has been discussed in relation to the 4A model and the various stages of the problem-solving process.

Divergent thought processes are characterised by:

- Free association of ideas
- The capacity to originate questions and ideas
- Making many from one
- Intuition
- Opening out

Convergent thought processes are characterised by:

- Logic and analysis
- Making one from many

- Mastery of detail
- Closing down

It hardly needs to be said, of course, that both are essential for effective and creative problem-solving.

The next scale is the *right brain–left brain* scale.

Our brains have two joined hemispheres, and each one operates in a quite different way.

The thought processes associated with the left brain are:

- Analytic
- Reductive
- Sequential
- Rational
- Fit information to existing models
- 'Vertical' thinking

The thought processes associated with the right brain are:

- Holistic
- Simultaneous
- Intuitive
- Pattern seeking
- Model creating
- Non-sequential
- 'Lateral' thinking

Two things should be pointed out. Firstly these characteristics suggest an association between right-brain thinking and divergence, and between left-brain thinking and convergence. They seem like different ways of describing the same thing.

Secondly, most people (those who are right-handed) are left-brain dominated. This suggests that they are more comfortable with the thought processes associated with left-brain and convergent thinking.

It seems to be true that our approach to most aspects of business life is dominated by left-brain, convergent approaches.

As we have said, both approaches are legitimate and necessary in the problem-solving process. Yet we tend to hide or even discourage right-brain/divergent thinking in the business context. It seems a pity that we don't reward this type of thinking. For many of us, one of the best ways to widen our own repertoire of skills is to practise and encourage more of the right-brain type thinking.

Take the following puzzles. Each one represents a well-known phrase or idea. It would be very difficult to arrive at the answer in any systematic or scientific way. You just need to allow your thoughts and ideas loose, and see what happens. Now you may also begin to appreciate why we included determination and the ability to 'stick at it' in our list of attributes earlier on!

1 VAD ERS   **2**   GET IT

                             GET IT

                             GET IT

                             GET IT

Summary

Today we have considered the skills that go towards making a successful problem-solver:

- A sound knowledge and experience base
- Personal ability and motivation levels
- Good heuristic skills
- Creativity

Here we have touched on ways of thinking to succeed at problem-solving. Tomorrow we will go on to explore in more depth styles of thinking and their influence on the way we tackle problems.

Thinking styles

Up to now we have considered the skills, techniques and processes concerned with problem-solving. On this final day we shall look at how our natural thinking style affects the way we tackle problems, and what we can learn about playing to our strengths and covering for our weaknesses.

We shall consider:

- Problem-solving styles
- Personality type
- Approaches to problem-solving

Problem-solving styles

We may not very often give ourselves the luxury of 'thinking about thinking'. However, our discussion on problem-solving skills and in particular about creativity, should convince us that there are varying ways to go about thinking. There we discussed some of the terms in common and informal usage that describe different ways of thinking.

We can conclude that:

- There are different ways of thinking
- People have preferences
- These might be related to our behaviour or personality style/type
- They affect the way we approach problem-solving
- Each kind of thinking is well adapted to certain kinds of problems and may be poorly adapted to other kinds of problems

We can illustrate using an example.

Add up the numbers from 1 to 10.

Now add up the numbers from 1 to 100.

Most people will solve the first problem by mechanically doing the sum:

1+2+3+4+5+6+7+8+9+10

Of course, this will not work easily with the second problem, and you may have to devise some sort of strategy or short cut to solve it.

One elegant solution is to line the numbers up in reverse order. Each pair adds up to 101, therefore the sum is 101 x 100 = 10100. The answer we require is half of this, i.e. 5500.

1	2	3	4	5	6 99	100	
100	99	98	97	96	95 2	1	+

101	101	101	101	101	101 101	101

In terms of preferences, many will be content with the steamroller approach to adding the numbers – as long as they then get the right answer. For other problems, there will be many approaches, although people rarely get one of these elegant solutions at first try. They have to be worked at: people have to look at the problem in a number of ways, trying things out, testing hunches and groping towards the answer.

It is also interesting that the elegant approaches can't be taught scientifically. However, we can learn to develop our skill with this kind of problem.

Another feature should be pointed out: people can develop a real facility for solving problems of this kind, e.g. with numbers, but they may not be able to translate these skills to other contexts. There are mathematicians who can't wire a plug!

This relates to the point made earlier in the week about the need for a knowledge or experience base. In the jargon, it can provide us with what is called 'metacognition'. This is a feeling, almost a 'sixth sense', or situational problem-solving capability in relation to the particular context.

It comes over time and experience, when we develop an almost unconscious understanding of the relationship between parts and an intimate knowledge of their functions.

Some of our old car mechanic friends have this incredible ability to diagnose problems from even the most inept description by the distressed customer. Of course, there are those who do not have this gift (they are the ones who usually get to fix my car!).

Personality type

Clearly, our thinking style is closely associated and influenced by our personality and our general approach to the world. Some information about these preferences is given by our personality type.

To give us an idea about these preferences, let us look at one of the most widely used personality instruments. This is the Myers–Briggs Type Indicator (MBTI). This inventory classifies people on a scale according to their preferences in each of four dimensions. The dimensions are:

Focus of attention
Extraversion – focus on the outer world of people and events
Introversion – focus on own inner world of experience

Mode of perception
Sensing – take information from their senses about the world
Intuition – focus on relationships between facts, connections, patterns

Making decisions
Thinking – logical, objective analysis
Feeling – person-centred focus

Orientation to outer world
Judging – planned, regulated, organised
Perceiving – flexible, spontaneous, adaptable

The scales look like this:

E _____ I

S _____ N

T _____ F

J _____ P

Your preferences in each of these four dimensions will give a characteristic type. For each of these there is a type description.

There is not space here to give a full description of the richness or usage of the model. Further information can be found in *Introduction to Type* by Isabel Briggs-Myers (Oxford Psychologists Press, 1993).

However, you can perhaps see that your preferences influence your thinking style. The most important scales for problem-solving are perception and decision-making.

S's tend to focus on real and actual concrete experience, to be pragmatic and to operate sequentially step by step. They may accept second-best solutions without exploring a wider range of possibilities.

N's tend to focus on the big picture, to be abstract, to be able to grasp pattern and possibility, complexity, change and energy. They might explore possibilities which have little basis in reality or fact.

T's tend to be analytical, logical and objective.

F's tend to be sympathetic, compassionate and accept value-based solutions.

The way you tackle problems will also be affected by your orientation preference.

J's tend to be scheduled, organised, systematic – good planners.

P's tend to be more spontaneous, open-ended, casual, flexible, curious.

It is also the case that certain kinds of questions and considerations operate at various stages of the problem-solving process.

S's will be good at laying out the basic information and facts of a problem.

N's will be good at finding new and novel ways of looking at a problem, inventing possibilities, or making unusual connections and spotting patterns.

In evaluating information, **T**'s will be good at logical thinking and objectively evaluating information. **F**'s will be good at judging the effects on people concerned and the fit with values.

As with all of these things, a good balance is necessary. You can use the above ideas to make judgements about where you think your preferences and strengths lie. Does it give you some insight about how you naturally go about certain kinds of problems?

The value of something like the MBTI is that it can help you to do this. It can also be used to give you an idea of approaches that you may be less comfortable with. If you think you may have a strong **T** preference, is it possible that you often fail to think of the consequences of the people aspects? Do you ignore their needs and values?

If you are a strong **S** (and there are lots of advantages to this), do you find it difficult to 'open out' your thinking, to 'think out of the box'?

Having a preference does not mean that you cannot discipline yourself and learn the skills and behaviour associated with the opposite preference. If you do this it will inevitably give you more options in problem situations.

Approaches to problem-solving

Creative modes of thinking
Some ideas have emerged from the work of neurolinguistic programming about styles of modes of thinking of highly creative people. A repertoire of creative strategies has emerged by studying how people like Walt Disney were so successful. It was found that they operate three distinct modes at different times and in different circumstances. These are:

The dreamer This is the green-field thinker, the creative 'off the wall', the generator of new ideas without regard to their practicality. Most thinking in this mode is done visually.

The critic This is the one who puts on the brakes. Typical statements are:

That won't work...
You can't do that because...

The realist This is the one who is pragmatic, is involved with what will work, how to do it, and implementation.

Many of us have a developed preference for one of these at the expense of the others. Of course, all of them are important, and highly creative people can operate them all at the appropriate time.

So a stereotypical dreamer will be good at generating ideas, but they may not be realistic, and may not work.

You might give some thought to your own preferences in terms of creative modes. It is possible to develop your repertoire by operating in unfamiliar ways.

If you find yourself always knocking new ideas down, for instance, you are likely to be a well-developed critic. Try giving the dreamer mode a chance – you may surprise yourself!

The Adapter-Innovator Scale (KAI)
Adaptors and innovators are two terms used by M. Kirton to describe personality/behaviour style in relation to management initiative and innovation in an organisational context (M.J. Kirton, *Adaptors and Innovators*, Routledge, 1989).

These two types approach the innovation/change process in quite different ways. The behaviour characteristics are:

Adaptors Precision, efficiency, use tried and trusted ideas, conformity, and method.

Innovators Think laterally, serve as a catalyst, query basic assumptions, and unconventional.

It should be said that these descriptions are at the extreme opposite ends of a single continuum. Most people score between these two extremes, and exhibit a balance of adaptive and innovative behaviour.

There are also strengths and disadvantages at any point on the continuum.

Adaptors and innovators also have beliefs and attitudes to the contrasting style. So innovators seem to believe that adaptors always conform to the status quo. Adaptors tend to strongly resist the ideas of the innovator.

It could be that these descriptions give you some insight into behaviour you have seen in your organisation. As with all style and type classifications, it is important to understand the nature of other people's behaviour.

Self-knowledge also helps us to know our own strengths and weaknesses, and to accept a balance of other styles and the contributions of others.

Summary

Today we have given considerable thought to styles of thinking and the ways in which they affect our approach to problem-solving. Models for personality types and modes of thinking are useful tools for analysing our strengths and weaknesses and allow us to take a critical perspective on and develop our own approach to problem-solving.

Throughout the week, therefore, we have looked at the skills, techniques, processes and appoaches related to problem-solving. The aim has been to enable you to distinguish between types of problems and to give you easy access to the skills and tools necessary to cope with a changing business environment. Remember that there is never any one way to solve a problem. Happy and successful problem-solving!'

4A The problem-solving model which incorporates the four stages of problem-solving: Agenda, Audit, Analysis, Action.

Action Fourth stage of problem-solving, which enables completion of the process through decision-making, implementation or further action.

Agenda Initial stage of problem-solving in which the problem is defined or criteria set.

Analysis Third stage of problem-solving. Use of logical techniques to converge on solution to problem.

Audit Second stage of problem-solving, used to diverge, build models, provide a map of the cause–effect processes.

Brainstorming Group problem-solving technique involving the generation of ideas.

Convergent–divergent Convergent – a mode of thinking that goes from the many to the one. Divergent – a mode of thinking that widens from the one to the many.

Heuristic The science of discovery and solving problems.

Kepner–Tregoe Inventors of rational management and the problem analysis approach that bears their name.

Mind map A visual method of mapping an information or concept space.

Pareto analysis Quantitative analysis of major factors in a problem situation.

PF problem Problem to find – a 'how to' or design-led problem.

Problem A situation with sub-optimal effects or outcomes involving some uncertainty.

Problem-solving The study of cause–effect processes in situations of uncertainty where there are actual or potential sub-optimal effects or outcomes.

PS problem Problem to solve – a problem where there is a deviation from some norm of unknown cause.

Right-brain–left-brain thinking Distinction of different types of thinking influenced by respective hemispheres of the brain.

Right-brain thinking – holistic, timeless.

Left-brain thinking – logical, sequential.